50 Premium Sugar Drink Recipes

By: Kelly Johnson

Table of Contents

- Classic Lemonade
- Raspberry Lime Rickey
- Watermelon Mint Cooler
- Pineapple Coconut Spritzer
- Strawberry Basil Lemonade
- Mango Lassi
- Blueberry Lemon Fizz
- Cherry Limeade
- Ginger Peach Iced Tea
- Iced Hibiscus Lemonade
- Coconut Water Lemonade
- Lemon Cucumber Cooler
- Blackberry Mojito Mocktail
- Pomegranate Iced Tea
- Watermelon Cooler
- Sparkling Lavender Lemonade
- Orange Mint Mojito
- Spiced Apple Cider
- Sparkling Cranberry Punch
- Kiwi Strawberry Fizz
- Coconut Mango Smoothie
- Pineapple Ginger Punch
- Honey Lemon Ginger Tea
- Peach Iced Tea Lemonade
- Lychee Mint Cooler
- Sweet Iced Matcha Latte
- Raspberry Mint Fizz
- Blueberry Mojito
- Lemon Ginger Sparkler
- Cantaloupe Basil Cooler
- Pineapple Mint Lemonade
- Apple Cinnamon Sparkler
- Sweetened Iced Chai
- Blackberry Lemon Fizz
- Passion Fruit Lemonade

- Lemon Lavender Iced Tea
- Orange Coconut Cream Soda
- Dragon Fruit Limeade
- Minty Green Tea Lemonade
- Sparkling Lemon Ginger Ale
- Pink Grapefruit Sparkler
- Cinnamon Apple Cooler
- Mango Pineapple Punch
- Plum Lemonade Fizz
- Lemon Peach Iced Tea
- Grapefruit Mint Fizz
- Guava Lime Cooler
- Watermelon Strawberry Punch
- Sweet Lemon Basil Spritz
- Blood Orange Fizz

Classic Lemonade

Ingredients:

- 1 cup fresh lemon juice
- 1 cup sugar
- 5 cups water
- Ice
- Lemon slices for garnish

Instructions:

1. In a saucepan, combine 1 cup of water with the sugar. Heat over medium heat until the sugar dissolves completely.
2. In a large pitcher, mix the simple syrup with the fresh lemon juice and the remaining 4 cups of water.
3. Stir well and adjust sweetness if necessary.
4. Serve over ice and garnish with lemon slices.

Raspberry Lime Rickey

Ingredients:

- 1 cup fresh raspberries
- 1/2 cup lime juice
- 2 tablespoons sugar
- 5 cups sparkling water
- Ice
- Lime slices and raspberries for garnish

Instructions:

1. In a small saucepan, heat raspberries and sugar until the raspberries break down and the sugar dissolves, about 5 minutes. Strain to remove seeds.
2. Combine the raspberry syrup with lime juice and sparkling water in a pitcher.
3. Add ice and stir well.
4. Garnish with lime slices and fresh raspberries.

Watermelon Mint Cooler

Ingredients:

- 3 cups watermelon, cubed
- 1/4 cup fresh mint leaves
- 2 tablespoons honey or sugar
- 2 cups water
- Ice
- Mint sprigs for garnish

Instructions:

1. Blend the watermelon and mint leaves until smooth.
2. Strain the juice through a fine mesh sieve into a pitcher.
3. Add water and sweeten with honey or sugar.
4. Serve over ice and garnish with mint sprigs.

Pineapple Coconut Spritzer

Ingredients:

- 1 cup pineapple juice
- 1/2 cup coconut water
- 1 tablespoon lime juice
- 2 cups sparkling water
- Ice
- Pineapple slices and mint for garnish

Instructions:

1. Combine pineapple juice, coconut water, and lime juice in a pitcher.
2. Add sparkling water and stir gently.
3. Serve over ice and garnish with pineapple slices and mint.

Strawberry Basil Lemonade

Ingredients:

- 1 cup fresh strawberries, hulled
- 1/4 cup fresh basil leaves
- 1 cup lemon juice
- 1/2 cup sugar
- 5 cups water
- Ice
- Basil sprigs and strawberry slices for garnish

Instructions:

1. Blend strawberries and basil leaves until smooth.
2. Strain the mixture to remove solids.
3. In a pitcher, combine the strawberry-basil juice with lemon juice, sugar, and water.
4. Serve over ice and garnish with basil sprigs and strawberry slices.

Mango Lassi

Ingredients:

- 1 cup fresh or frozen mango
- 1 cup yogurt
- 1/2 cup milk
- 1 tablespoon honey or sugar
- A pinch of ground cardamom (optional)
- Ice cubes

Instructions:

1. Blend the mango, yogurt, milk, honey, and cardamom until smooth.
2. Add ice cubes and blend again until chilled.
3. Serve immediately.

Blueberry Lemon Fizz

Ingredients:

- 1 cup fresh blueberries
- 1/2 cup lemon juice
- 2 tablespoons honey or sugar
- 2 cups sparkling water
- Ice
- Lemon slices and blueberries for garnish

Instructions:

1. In a blender, combine blueberries, lemon juice, and honey.
2. Strain the mixture through a fine mesh sieve to remove solids.
3. Add the blueberry syrup to sparkling water and stir gently.
4. Serve over ice and garnish with lemon slices and blueberries.

Cherry Limeade

Ingredients:

- 1 cup fresh cherries, pitted
- 1/2 cup lime juice
- 2 tablespoons sugar
- 4 cups sparkling water
- Ice
- Lime wedges and cherries for garnish

Instructions:

1. Blend the cherries and sugar until smooth, then strain through a fine sieve.
2. Mix the cherry syrup with lime juice and sparkling water in a pitcher.
3. Serve over ice and garnish with lime wedges and cherries.

Ginger Peach Iced Tea

Ingredients:

- 2 ripe peaches, sliced
- 1 tablespoon fresh ginger, grated
- 4 cups brewed black tea, cooled
- 2 tablespoons honey or sugar
- Ice
- Peach slices for garnish

Instructions:

1. Blend the peaches and grated ginger, then strain to remove solids.
2. Mix the peach-ginger juice with the brewed tea and sweeten with honey.
3. Serve over ice and garnish with peach slices.

Iced Hibiscus Lemonade

Ingredients:

- 1/2 cup dried hibiscus flowers
- 1 cup lemon juice
- 1/2 cup sugar
- 5 cups water
- Ice
- Lemon slices for garnish

Instructions:

1. Steep the dried hibiscus flowers in boiling water for 5 minutes, then strain.
2. Combine the hibiscus tea with lemon juice and sugar in a pitcher.
3. Add cold water and stir well.
4. Serve over ice and garnish with lemon slices.

Coconut Water Lemonade

Ingredients:

- 1 cup fresh coconut water
- 1/2 cup lemon juice
- 2 tablespoons honey or sugar (optional)
- 3 cups water
- Ice
- Lemon slices for garnish

Instructions:

1. In a pitcher, combine coconut water, lemon juice, and honey (if using).
2. Add water and stir until well mixed.
3. Serve over ice and garnish with lemon slices.

Lemon Cucumber Cooler

Ingredients:

- 1 cucumber, sliced
- 1/2 cup lemon juice
- 2 tablespoons honey or agave syrup
- 3 cups cold water
- Ice
- Cucumber slices and lemon wedges for garnish

Instructions:

1. In a blender, blend the cucumber slices and honey until smooth.
2. Strain the mixture into a pitcher, discarding the solids.
3. Add lemon juice and cold water, stirring well.
4. Serve over ice and garnish with cucumber slices and lemon wedges.

Blackberry Mojito Mocktail

Ingredients:

- 1/2 cup blackberries
- 10 fresh mint leaves
- 1 tablespoon lime juice
- 2 teaspoons sugar or honey
- 1 cup sparkling water
- Ice
- Mint sprigs and blackberries for garnish

Instructions:

1. Muddle the blackberries, mint leaves, lime juice, and sugar in a glass to release the flavors.
2. Add ice and top with sparkling water.
3. Stir gently and garnish with mint sprigs and blackberries.

Pomegranate Iced Tea

Ingredients:

- 2 cups pomegranate juice
- 4 cups brewed black tea, cooled
- 1 tablespoon honey or sugar (optional)
- Ice
- Pomegranate seeds for garnish

Instructions:

1. Combine the pomegranate juice, brewed tea, and honey (if desired) in a pitcher.
2. Stir well to dissolve the sweetener.
3. Serve over ice and garnish with pomegranate seeds.

Watermelon Cooler

Ingredients:

- 3 cups watermelon, cubed
- 1 tablespoon lime juice
- 1 tablespoon honey or sugar (optional)
- 1 cup cold water
- Ice
- Lime wedges for garnish

Instructions:

1. Blend the watermelon with lime juice and honey until smooth.
2. Strain the mixture to remove any pulp.
3. Add cold water and stir to combine.
4. Serve over ice and garnish with lime wedges.

Sparkling Lavender Lemonade

Ingredients:

- 1 tablespoon dried lavender buds
- 1 cup lemon juice
- 1/2 cup honey or sugar
- 4 cups sparkling water
- Ice
- Lemon slices for garnish

Instructions:

1. In a small pot, simmer lavender buds with 1 cup of water to make lavender syrup. Strain and let cool.
2. In a pitcher, combine lemon juice, lavender syrup, and honey or sugar.
3. Add sparkling water and stir gently.
4. Serve over ice and garnish with lemon slices.

Orange Mint Mojito

Ingredients:

- 1/2 cup fresh orange juice
- 10 mint leaves
- 1 tablespoon lime juice
- 1 teaspoon honey or sugar
- 1 cup sparkling water
- Ice
- Orange slices and mint sprigs for garnish

Instructions:

1. Muddle the mint leaves, orange juice, lime juice, and honey in a glass.
2. Add ice and top with sparkling water.
3. Stir gently and garnish with orange slices and mint sprigs.

Spiced Apple Cider

Ingredients:

- 4 cups apple cider
- 2 cinnamon sticks
- 3-4 cloves
- 1 orange, sliced
- 1 tablespoon honey (optional)
- Ice

Instructions:

1. In a pot, heat the apple cider, cinnamon sticks, cloves, and orange slices over medium heat.
2. Simmer for 10-15 minutes to allow the flavors to infuse.
3. Strain the cider and add honey, if desired.
4. Serve hot or chilled over ice.

Sparkling Cranberry Punch

Ingredients:

- 2 cups cranberry juice
- 1 cup orange juice
- 1 tablespoon lime juice
- 2 cups sparkling water
- Ice
- Cranberries and lime slices for garnish

Instructions:

1. In a pitcher, combine cranberry juice, orange juice, and lime juice.
2. Add sparkling water and stir gently.
3. Serve over ice and garnish with cranberries and lime slices.

Kiwi Strawberry Fizz

Ingredients:

- 2 ripe kiwis, peeled
- 1 cup strawberries, hulled
- 1 tablespoon lime juice
- 2 teaspoons honey or sugar (optional)
- 2 cups sparkling water
- Ice
- Strawberry slices and kiwi slices for garnish

Instructions:

1. Blend the kiwis, strawberries, lime juice, and honey until smooth.
2. Strain the mixture into a pitcher to remove the pulp.
3. Add sparkling water and stir gently.
4. Serve over ice and garnish with strawberry slices and kiwi slices.

Coconut Mango Smoothie

Ingredients:

- 1 ripe mango, peeled and chopped
- 1/2 cup coconut milk
- 1/2 cup Greek yogurt
- 1 tablespoon honey or agave syrup
- Ice cubes

Instructions:

1. In a blender, combine the mango, coconut milk, Greek yogurt, and honey.
2. Blend until smooth and creamy.
3. Add ice cubes and blend again until frothy.
4. Serve immediately and garnish with a mango slice if desired.

Pineapple Ginger Punch

Ingredients:

- 2 cups pineapple juice
- 1 tablespoon fresh ginger, grated
- 1 tablespoon lime juice
- 1 teaspoon honey or sugar (optional)
- Sparkling water
- Ice
- Pineapple slices for garnish

Instructions:

1. In a shaker or large glass, combine pineapple juice, grated ginger, lime juice, and honey.
2. Shake or stir well to mix.
3. Pour over ice and top with sparkling water.
4. Garnish with pineapple slices and serve.

Honey Lemon Ginger Tea

Ingredients:

- 1 tablespoon fresh ginger, grated
- 1 tablespoon honey
- 1 tablespoon lemon juice
- 2 cups hot water
- Lemon slices for garnish

Instructions:

1. Boil the water and pour it over the grated ginger in a teapot or mug.
2. Stir in honey and lemon juice.
3. Let it steep for about 5 minutes, then strain.
4. Serve hot with lemon slices as garnish.

Peach Iced Tea Lemonade

Ingredients:

- 2 cups brewed black tea, chilled
- 1 cup peach juice
- 1/2 cup lemon juice
- 1-2 tablespoons honey or sugar (optional)
- Ice
- Peach slices and lemon wedges for garnish

Instructions:

1. In a pitcher, combine the chilled tea, peach juice, lemon juice, and honey (if desired).
2. Stir well and adjust sweetness to taste.
3. Serve over ice and garnish with peach slices and lemon wedges.

Lychee Mint Cooler

Ingredients:

- 1 cup canned lychee, drained
- 10 fresh mint leaves
- 1 tablespoon lime juice
- 1 tablespoon honey or sugar (optional)
- 2 cups cold water
- Ice
- Mint sprigs and lychee for garnish

Instructions:

1. In a blender, combine lychee, mint leaves, lime juice, and honey.
2. Add cold water and blend until smooth.
3. Strain if desired, and serve over ice.
4. Garnish with mint sprigs and lychee.

Sweet Iced Matcha Latte

Ingredients:

- 1 teaspoon matcha powder
- 1 tablespoon hot water
- 1/2 cup milk (or plant-based milk)
- 1 tablespoon honey or sweetener of choice
- Ice

Instructions:

1. In a small bowl, whisk matcha powder and hot water until smooth and frothy.
2. In a glass, combine matcha mixture with milk and sweetener.
3. Stir well and serve over ice.

Raspberry Mint Fizz

Ingredients:

- 1/2 cup fresh raspberries
- 1 tablespoon fresh mint leaves
- 1 tablespoon lime juice
- 1 tablespoon honey or sugar (optional)
- 2 cups sparkling water
- Ice
- Mint sprigs and raspberries for garnish

Instructions:

1. Muddle the raspberries, mint leaves, lime juice, and honey in a glass to release the flavors.
2. Add ice and top with sparkling water.
3. Stir gently and garnish with mint sprigs and raspberries.

Blueberry Mojito

Ingredients:

- 1/2 cup fresh blueberries
- 10 fresh mint leaves
- 1 tablespoon lime juice
- 1 teaspoon honey or sugar
- 1 cup sparkling water
- Ice
- Blueberries and mint sprigs for garnish

Instructions:

1. Muddle the blueberries, mint leaves, lime juice, and honey in a glass.
2. Add ice and top with sparkling water.
3. Stir gently and garnish with blueberries and mint sprigs.

Lemon Ginger Sparkler

Ingredients:

- 1 tablespoon fresh ginger, grated
- 2 tablespoons lemon juice
- 1 tablespoon honey or agave syrup
- 2 cups sparkling water
- Ice
- Lemon slices and ginger for garnish

Instructions:

1. In a glass, combine grated ginger, lemon juice, and honey.
2. Add ice and top with sparkling water.
3. Stir gently and garnish with lemon slices and fresh ginger.

Cantaloupe Basil Cooler

Ingredients:

- 2 cups cantaloupe, cubed
- 10 fresh basil leaves
- 1 tablespoon lime juice
- 1 teaspoon honey or sugar (optional)
- 2 cups cold water
- Ice
- Basil leaves and cantaloupe for garnish

Instructions:

1. Blend the cantaloupe, basil leaves, lime juice, and honey until smooth.
2. Strain the mixture if desired, and add cold water.
3. Serve over ice and garnish with basil leaves and cantaloupe cubes.

Pineapple Mint Lemonade

Ingredients:

- 2 cups pineapple juice
- 1/4 cup fresh mint leaves
- 1 tablespoon lime juice
- 1 tablespoon honey or agave syrup (optional)
- Sparkling water
- Ice
- Pineapple slices and mint leaves for garnish

Instructions:

1. In a blender, combine pineapple juice, mint leaves, lime juice, and honey.
2. Blend until smooth, then strain if desired.
3. Serve over ice and top with sparkling water.
4. Garnish with pineapple slices and mint leaves.

Apple Cinnamon Sparkler

Ingredients:

- 1 cup apple juice
- 1/2 teaspoon ground cinnamon
- 1 tablespoon honey or maple syrup (optional)
- Sparkling water
- Ice
- Apple slices and cinnamon stick for garnish

Instructions:

1. In a glass, combine apple juice, ground cinnamon, and honey.
2. Stir well to dissolve the cinnamon.
3. Add ice and top with sparkling water.
4. Garnish with apple slices and a cinnamon stick.

Sweetened Iced Chai

Ingredients:

- 2 chai tea bags
- 1 cup boiling water
- 1 tablespoon honey or sugar (optional)
- 1/2 cup milk (or plant-based milk)
- Ice
- Cinnamon stick or ground cinnamon for garnish

Instructions:

1. Brew the chai tea bags in boiling water for 5-7 minutes.
2. Stir in honey or sugar to sweeten.
3. Let the tea cool and pour over ice.
4. Add milk and stir.
5. Garnish with a cinnamon stick or sprinkle of ground cinnamon.

Blackberry Lemon Fizz

Ingredients:

- 1/2 cup fresh blackberries
- 1 tablespoon lemon juice
- 1 tablespoon honey or agave syrup
- Sparkling water
- Ice
- Lemon slices and blackberries for garnish

Instructions:

1. Muddle the blackberries, lemon juice, and honey in a glass.
2. Add ice and top with sparkling water.
3. Stir gently and garnish with lemon slices and blackberries.

Passion Fruit Lemonade

Ingredients:

- 1/2 cup passion fruit pulp (or 1/4 cup juice)
- 2 tablespoons lemon juice
- 2 tablespoons honey or sugar (optional)
- 2 cups cold water
- Ice
- Lemon wedges for garnish

Instructions:

1. In a pitcher, combine passion fruit pulp, lemon juice, and honey.
2. Add cold water and stir to mix.
3. Serve over ice and garnish with lemon wedges.

Lemon Lavender Iced Tea

Ingredients:

- 2 black tea bags
- 1 tablespoon dried lavender flowers
- 1 tablespoon honey or sugar (optional)
- 1/4 cup fresh lemon juice
- Ice
- Lemon slices and lavender sprigs for garnish

Instructions:

1. Brew the black tea with dried lavender flowers for 5 minutes.
2. Remove the tea bags and lavender, then stir in honey and lemon juice.
3. Let the tea cool and pour over ice.
4. Garnish with lemon slices and lavender sprigs.

Orange Coconut Cream Soda

Ingredients:

- 1 cup orange juice
- 1/4 cup coconut cream
- 1 teaspoon vanilla extract
- Sparkling water
- Ice
- Orange slices for garnish

Instructions:

1. In a glass, combine orange juice, coconut cream, and vanilla extract.
2. Stir well until smooth.
3. Add ice and top with sparkling water.
4. Garnish with orange slices.

Dragon Fruit Limeade

Ingredients:

- 1/2 cup dragon fruit (frozen or fresh, peeled)
- 2 tablespoons lime juice
- 1 tablespoon honey or agave syrup
- 2 cups cold water
- Ice
- Lime wedges and dragon fruit for garnish

Instructions:

1. Blend the dragon fruit, lime juice, and honey until smooth.
2. Add cold water and stir well.
3. Serve over ice and garnish with lime wedges and dragon fruit.

Minty Green Tea Lemonade

Ingredients:

- 2 green tea bags
- 1/4 cup fresh mint leaves
- 1/4 cup lemon juice
- 1 tablespoon honey or agave syrup
- 2 cups cold water
- Ice
- Lemon slices and mint sprigs for garnish

Instructions:

1. Brew the green tea bags in hot water and let it steep for 3-5 minutes.
2. Add fresh mint leaves and stir in honey to sweeten.
3. Let it cool, then mix in lemon juice and cold water.
4. Serve over ice and garnish with lemon slices and mint sprigs.

Sparkling Lemon Ginger Ale

Ingredients:

- 1/2 cup freshly squeezed lemon juice
- 1/2 teaspoon grated ginger
- 1 tablespoon honey or agave syrup (optional)
- Sparkling water
- Ice
- Lemon slices and mint sprigs for garnish

Instructions:

1. In a glass, combine lemon juice, grated ginger, and honey.
2. Stir well to dissolve the honey.
3. Add ice and top with sparkling water.
4. Garnish with lemon slices and mint sprigs.

Pink Grapefruit Sparkler

Ingredients:

- 1 cup pink grapefruit juice
- 1 tablespoon lime juice
- 1 tablespoon honey or sugar (optional)
- Sparkling water
- Ice
- Grapefruit slices for garnish

Instructions:

1. In a glass, mix together pink grapefruit juice, lime juice, and honey.
2. Stir to combine and dissolve the honey.
3. Fill the glass with ice and top with sparkling water.
4. Garnish with grapefruit slices.

Cinnamon Apple Cooler

Ingredients:

- 1 cup apple juice
- 1/2 teaspoon ground cinnamon
- 1 tablespoon lemon juice
- Sparkling water
- Ice
- Apple slices and cinnamon stick for garnish

Instructions:

1. In a glass, combine apple juice, cinnamon, and lemon juice.
2. Stir well to ensure the cinnamon is fully dissolved.
3. Add ice and top with sparkling water.
4. Garnish with apple slices and a cinnamon stick.

Mango Pineapple Punch

Ingredients:

- 1/2 cup mango puree
- 1/2 cup pineapple juice
- 1 tablespoon lime juice
- 1 tablespoon honey or agave syrup (optional)
- Sparkling water
- Ice
- Pineapple and mango chunks for garnish

Instructions:

1. In a shaker or blender, combine mango puree, pineapple juice, lime juice, and honey.
2. Shake or blend until smooth.
3. Serve over ice and top with sparkling water.
4. Garnish with pineapple and mango chunks.

Plum Lemonade Fizz

Ingredients:

- 1/2 cup plum puree (or plum juice)
- 1/4 cup lemon juice
- 1 tablespoon honey or sugar (optional)
- Sparkling water
- Ice
- Plum slices and mint sprigs for garnish

Instructions:

1. In a blender, combine plums, lemon juice, and honey, and blend until smooth.
2. Strain the mixture if desired, then pour over ice.
3. Top with sparkling water.
4. Garnish with plum slices and mint sprigs.

Lemon Peach Iced Tea

Ingredients:

- 2 black tea bags
- 1/2 cup fresh peach puree or peach juice
- 1/4 cup fresh lemon juice
- 1 tablespoon honey or sugar (optional)
- Ice
- Lemon slices and peach wedges for garnish

Instructions:

1. Brew the black tea with tea bags for 3-5 minutes.
2. Stir in honey, then let the tea cool to room temperature.
3. Add fresh peach puree and lemon juice.
4. Serve over ice and garnish with lemon slices and peach wedges.

Grapefruit Mint Fizz

Ingredients:

- 1 cup freshly squeezed grapefruit juice
- 1 tablespoon lime juice
- 1 tablespoon honey or agave syrup (optional)
- Sparkling water
- Fresh mint leaves
- Ice
- Grapefruit slices and mint sprigs for garnish

Instructions:

1. In a glass, combine grapefruit juice, lime juice, and honey. Stir to dissolve the honey.
2. Add ice and top with sparkling water.
3. Gently slap mint leaves between your hands to release the oils and add them to the glass.
4. Garnish with grapefruit slices and mint sprigs.

Guava Lime Cooler

Ingredients:

- 1/2 cup guava juice or puree
- 1 tablespoon lime juice
- 1 tablespoon honey or sugar (optional)
- Sparkling water
- Ice
- Lime wedges for garnish

Instructions:

1. In a glass, mix together guava juice, lime juice, and honey or sugar.
2. Stir until the sweetener is dissolved.
3. Add ice and top with sparkling water.
4. Garnish with lime wedges.

Watermelon Strawberry Punch

Ingredients:

- 1 cup watermelon puree
- 1/2 cup strawberry puree
- 1 tablespoon lime juice
- 1 tablespoon honey or sugar (optional)
- Sparkling water
- Ice
- Fresh watermelon and strawberry slices for garnish

Instructions:

1. In a blender, combine watermelon and strawberry puree with lime juice and honey or sugar.
2. Blend until smooth and strain if needed.
3. Pour the mixture into a glass filled with ice.
4. Top with sparkling water.
5. Garnish with fresh watermelon and strawberry slices.

Sweet Lemon Basil Spritz

Ingredients:

- 1/2 cup lemon juice
- 1 tablespoon honey or agave syrup
- Fresh basil leaves
- Sparkling water
- Ice
- Lemon slices and basil sprigs for garnish

Instructions:

1. In a glass, combine lemon juice and honey, stirring until the honey dissolves.
2. Gently muddle fresh basil leaves in the glass to release their flavor.
3. Add ice and top with sparkling water.
4. Garnish with lemon slices and basil sprigs.

Blood Orange Fizz

Ingredients:

- 1 cup blood orange juice
- 1 tablespoon lime juice
- 1 tablespoon honey or sugar (optional)
- Sparkling water
- Ice
- Blood orange slices for garnish

Instructions:

1. In a glass, combine blood orange juice, lime juice, and honey or sugar.
2. Stir well to dissolve the honey or sugar.
3. Add ice and top with sparkling water.
4. Garnish with blood orange slices.

www.ingramcontent.com/pod-product-compliance
Lightning Source LLC
LaVergne TN
LVHW081501060526
838201LV00056BA/2871